articulate
AT WORK

How Performance
Techniques Bring Business
Communication to Life

Hilary Blair
Robin A. Miller, PhD

*Articulate at Work: How Performance Techniques Bring
Business Communication to Life*
Published by ArticulateRC Press
Denver, CO

ISBN: 978-1-7361096-0-1

Business Communication / Meetings & Presentation

Cover by Tasha Brown
Interior design by Wolf Design & Marketing
Illustrations © Teresa Logan

QUANTITY PURCHASES: Schools, companies, professional groups, clubs, and other organizations may qualify
for special terms when ordering quantities of this title.
For information, email office@articulaterc.com.

artICULATE**RC**
PRESS

CONTENTS

PROLOGUE

Acting is about being real in imaginary circumstances. Business is about being real in *real* circumstances. That's what makes it hard.

~Hilary Blair, CEO ARTiculate Real&Clear

CONNECTING THEATRE AND BUSINESS

THE THEATRE is the ultimate training ground for business and professional communication. Does that seem obvious? It wasn't to me. It had to be pointed out, and I had to be immersed in the business world before I could see the connection. Even then, it took time for the rather large chip I was carrying on my shoulder to erode.

I realized I was thoroughly enjoying this new world that I had overlooked as a performer—a world hungry for communication skills and an artistic approach. As a performer, I had caved to the belief that all business and moneymaking schemes were mind-numbing and evil, when, in reality, they were parts of a thriving economy that create an intricate conduit for moving energy and ideas. Likewise, the theatre is in the business of moving energy and ideas. Similar processes exist in both worlds. If it's hard to imagine how the theatre can offer real value to you in business, ask yourself why. Have you bought into the concept that the arts are frivolous and performers are fake?

For more than thirty-five years, I've been immersed in the theatre as a performer, director, writer, and teacher. The connection between the business world and the theatre world wasn't easy for me to see. It was Nell Merlino, an inspiring business visionary, who created the bridge from the theatre to the business world for this tried-and-true theatre and voice teacher. She saw me in a play as a tomato, *Tomato Plant Girl* and connected my artistic aptitude with helping the business world embrace its individual greatness.

Based on her encouragement, a whole new world opened up. I became increasingly aware that business runs the world. I also saw that despite its mastery of meeting consumer needs, expertly moving money, creating systems, and measuring and tracking, the business world was less effective in developing self-awareness, communication, and flexibility—the very essence of theatre training. The artistic world is where the human, the performer, is awakened and where the performer's skills are practiced and honed.

The best performers know that to be effective in the production or the final concert, they have to sharpen their skills. Similarly, for business, each person works on various skills/tasks individually, and when individual skills/tasks interlink for the overall goal or purpose of the business, the business succeeds. The interlinking of artistic practice and the business world can create real and clear communication that's essential to connection and moving relationships, energy, and ideas forward.

Performers study and work to be in the moment and be present. It's a common misunderstanding that performers are being fake while acting, when in fact, they are practicing to be realistically present in each moment. The energy we often see as fake is as equally undesirable in acting as it is in public presentation. As an audience, we want the wall to come down so that we can connect to the presenter. As the presenter, this process can be the scariest step: to be open, available ... and connected. At ARTiculate: Real&Clear, we work to align the speaking voice with the expressive voice for effective connection and communication style.

FINDING THE RHYTHM OF COMMUNICATION

Everything is communication. From a musical performance perspective, we're creating meaning with every touch of the piano keys to every sound of the voice. Slight shifts in any of these will create a new meaning for our audience.

To control our communication, we need awareness. To make changes, we have to know how our voice, our message, and our nonverbals are landing on our audience. Yes, even in performance, these key elements are either working for our connection or hindering our connection with the audience.

For years, I worked in an environment where I was told that I needed to shift my communication style. Sandwich the message; don't say the message; soften the message. Part of what I was running into was culture and fit, and yet, there was a strand of truth in the advice. I could shift an approach so that the landing worked better to be heard. The problem was that I didn't know how to do that in a way that honored my communication style and my values.

So, as any musician would, I continued to practice, and I approached my communication differently. Our communication and interactions have a lasting impact. Musicians and actors connect to works emotionally; they'll think of events or feelings from the past/present, reconnect to those moments so they can apply the past emotion to a current moment, and bring their art form to life. We also analyze the text in an attempt to reconnect to the librettist's or composer's intent. Sometimes, we find ourselves looking to the past to inform the current moment.

Prior moments precede and color one's approach. Sometimes we learn best how to shift our communication through this retrospective approach. We remember what did or didn't work. We can learn from our past and reconnect with it in the present and shift what hasn't been working in our favor.

WHAT'S THIS
BOOK ABOUT?

We've gathered some of the thoughts shared as blogs over the past few years. Our goal, as co-authors, is to give a structure to the concepts and make them actionable for you in the business world. For example, interviewing for a job can get laden with past history. Lighten your attitude with the new perspective of the audition. Thinking about an interview as an audition similarly can be a reframing tool for improved attitude and growth.

Whether through the lens of the theatre world or the music world, enjoy the reframe and may the lens of the performer enhance your authenticity and communication connections. Getting real in your business communication is a journey, and we invite you to be curious and questioning, introspective and experimental as you explore ideas and try them on.

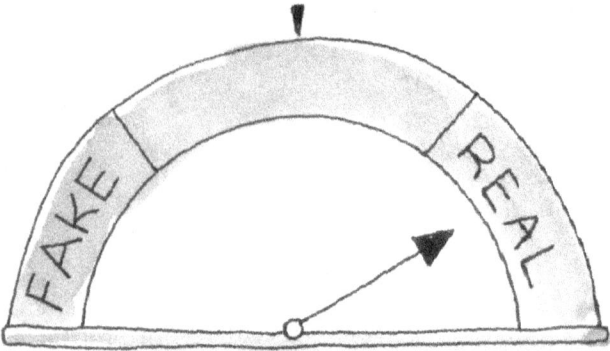

SCENE 1

WHY THEATRE?

HARNESS YOUR PROFESSIONAL PERFORMER

COMMUNICATION IN BUSINESS involves a lot of presenting, discussing, and persuading. Similar needs are noted in public speaking. So, you want to be the best public speaker you can, right? But why would you choose a trained performer to help finesse your next keynote or presentation?

You may think: "Won't I be learning how to be fake?" "Won't it be about acting, which makes me feel vulnerable and uncomfortable?" "I don't need to act. I just need to get the information across."

Others will realize: "Professional performers are

experts in story, voice, nonverbal communication, movement, creativity, character, collaboration, receiving feedback, taking risks, and meeting deadlines!"

Let's clear up a few key points.

Acting isn't about being "fake." Acting is about being real. Performers train to be present by working through imaginary situations. Performers don't bother studying how to be fake, because naturally we all are fairly decent at being fake (or inauthentic) on our own.

Performers study how to use voice and body most effectively in service of the story being told while taking into account the audience receiving it. This dual focus works collaboratively toward a common goal. Performers study how to be, and remain, present and real.

Trained professional performers (singers, dancers, etc.) have exercises and techniques designed to train them to remain in the moment—to be present. These techniques can translate as tips and tricks to help any professional communicate more easily and effectively.

Performers with teaching, coaching, and directing experience also have a highly developed sense of when experiences are fake, what might be causing this, and how to get clients connected to real outcomes so these fake things don't get in the way of the delivery. Part of the process of rehearsal for a performer involves being aware of when they're connected and being real, as well as when they're disconnected from the truth of the moment. This is brought to the artist's attention when a director senses a lack of connection or commitment. Sometimes performers can adjust on their own, but often need an outside eye for guidance.

In addition to being sensitive to the "fake-meter," trained performers are also comfortable with diving into what makes people tick (the "why" of things) without going into therapy. It's a character study, not a personal dissection or triage. Coaches, trainers, and facilitators who are also professional performers are often powerful teachers. As a side note, any skilled coach knows the line between therapy and therapeutic and won't cross it.

Being a great public speaker means constantly refining your techniques. It's the same with being a great leader. Beyond this, an excellent performer must work well with others toward a shared end goal. Being an excellent leader means heading up a team that works collaboratively to successfully create a product that's useful and profitable.

LET'S PLAY SHOW AND TELL

Remember show and tell? That improvisational experience when perhaps your parents wished there had been a rehearsed script? It was fun, right? The good news is that it was also a great training ground for improving your public speaking ability.

I created some of my best memories during kindergarten show and tell time. I would spend hours thinking about what I would bring and how I would describe it to my five-year-old classmates. It was a very serious decision for this kindergartner. One week, I was particularly inspired. I wanted my item to stand out from all the others. I wanted my treasure to be special. As I went out the front door, I placed in my pocket a tiny brown pill bottle with a round rock in it. When my name was called, I proudly displayed this fantastic object. My teacher, Mrs. Morrison, and my classmates listened with rapt attention as I talked about my mom going into the hospital to have a gallstone removed. I felt so lucky that she had brought it home from the hospital—preserving it for all time!

When I returned home and told my mom what I'd taken to show and tell, she was horrified. A few weeks earlier, I'd sung a questionable song for show and tell, and this, combined with the gallstone incident, inspired my mom to implement an "Is it appropriate?" test before giving me approval to share something.

I look back on these times with great joy because show and tell was so much fun! It was my first experience of standing up in public to give a presentation. What has changed since then? And why has it changed? To find out, let's consider what I learned.

It's important to take time to think about what

you're going to present. It should be something that inspires you, or at least that you think is pretty cool. My choice of topic may have had an unexpected effect on others. Similarly, some presentations need to be brainstormed and planned so we don't stumble into a presentation hole.

Our presentations, if planned and chosen appropriately, can live in the minds of others, as well as our own, for a long time. Our presentations can influence others for a greater cause and continue to live beyond the moment when we take the stage or present in a boardroom. Often, I wonder if Mrs. Morrison remembers my show and tell presentations and if she smiles.

Perhaps most importantly, I don't remember being nervous or concerned about what my classmates would think. I just stood up and boldly shared a topic that I knew very well. I shared a story that had impacted my young, naive life, assured that others would be just as interested.

Why can't public speaking feel like that now? Before you get lost in an explanation about how much more intense your work is now compared to kindergarten, pause and ask yourself: Is it really? Or did someone somewhere along the line make you feel like it had to be hard and nerve-wracking to speak in front of groups so that now you consider it to be work? Maybe it feels like work because you don't want to appear too eager to take the spotlight. How much easier is it for your audience to hear what you have to say if you like what you're talking about and enjoy being there? Is citing numbers for a CFO any less exciting than seeing a gallstone when you're five years old? It's your enthusiasm and interest in the subject that matters. That's how you connect with your audience.

Ultimately, show and tell was fun! And it still can be a pleasure to share your ideas and get feedback from your audience. It doesn't have to be hard nor painful to present in order to be effective nor to be taken seriously. When you enjoy show and tell time—whether you prepare the script or improvise—your audience will, too.

DIVING INTO PUBLIC SPEAKING

Like many professional business leaders, odds are good that you're moving into Act II of your career and your life. You want to share your message and your ideas because you know that you've something important to say—something that audiences will benefit from knowing—or you've developed an expertise that others want to hear about. You're ready to connect with people in a new way. Clearly, this isn't an ending. It's simply the next phase. Your timing couldn't be better because in Act I, you set everything up to prepare you for this big, bold step. Perhaps it was almost formulaic: undergraduate program, graduate

program, job, family, promotion. Now you're looking at what you've done, rethinking, reworking, and
recommitting. The possibilities abound, including
having your voice heard, whether it's connected to
your current job or not.

Our advice: Do it. We meet many presenters at
this juncture. Wisely, they approach a company like
ARTiculate: Real&Clear because they want to find,
unearth, and create the best keynotes to share with
the world. Or they're polishing their speaking skills to
take it to the next level, kicking it up a notch.

Public speaking is a powerful platform, provid-
ing a place for individuals to share their experience
and ideas and leave their footprint on the world. If
one person can move another person to shift their
perspective on business or life, they've created a
ripple effect that moves others and moves the world.
So let's get started.

Begin by gathering your thoughts about what
you want to speak about. Write down all the topics
you'd like to speak about, no matter how incomplete
they may seem. Just get it all down on paper. Another
option is to speak your ideas into a recorder if you feel
limited by the writing process. Remember, the goal is
to be as free and creative as you can. Don't edit yourself or overthink how people will receive your ideas.
Just get them all out.

Take a public speaking class in person or virtually.
Plenty of courses exist in cities around the country,

and they're a great way to help you overcome what holds you back in terms of public speaking—especially nerves. Toastmasters International is a great option, for they have 292,000 members in more than 14,350 clubs in 122 countries. Odds are good there's a chapter near you! If you have the opportunity, hire a speaking coach. One-on-one sessions are invaluable, and a good coach will help you create your speech and work with you on the delivery, too.

Practice, practice, practice, wherever you can. Speak whenever you can—at work, at the clubs you belong to, and to nonprofit groups that want to hear what you have to say. From here, you'll be able to leverage your experience as a speaker and, if it's your goal, eventually get paid to speak. Also check out the National Speakers Association, a great source for community, education, and entrepreneurial business knowledge that can help you find success in the speaking profession. The goal is to give speeches regularly in front of a group of your peers. The rule of thumb is that practice makes perfect. Well, maybe perfect practice makes perfect ... but practice will allow you to improve.

Here's to your Act 2! The curtain is rising. Take the stage and let your voice be heard—connect.

SCENE 2

THE AUDITION: INTERVIEWS AND BUSINESS PITCHES

A GOOD FIT

ARE YOU RIGHT FOR THE ROLE? Are you right for the job or task? In the theatre, the audition is the process of showing up and sharing a small, prepared/scripted piece or improvised material, usually in competition with a larger group of individuals, to prove you're the best fit for the job. It's an art, knowing your type and figuring out how to present yourself in a way that the casting directors can see you successfully filling the role. Performers do their best to show they'll be the top choice by preparing their audition material thoroughly and then thoughtfully choosing clothes, hair, accessories, and grooming. Going more deeply, they work on the voice, the clarity of the message, and their nonverbals and physicality.

It's the same in business. Make it easy for your audience to understand what you have to offer. Show up fully. Don't sell something or someone you aren't, but take the prep seriously. Knowing how to show your strengths and make a good first impression is essential to auditioning.

THE BUSINESS PITCH

Preparing to deliver a business pitch is similar to preparing for an audition, the key word being "prepare." Preparation can make the difference between nailing the part/getting new business or blowing it. For an acting gig, auditions are your opportunity to demonstrate that you're the best performer for the part. At an audition, you may be called into a room to do a monologue or read sides with another performer (or non-actor), and your performance may be taped. Auditions are odd because the material you read may bear little resemblance to the actual acting gig.

Likewise, your skill at delivering a business pitch to a potential client often has little resemblance to the work you'll do together. You'll need to be ready with a pitch at networking events and casual interactions, as well as at competitions and meetings with your bankers or potential clients. Think of your business pitch as if it were an audition for new business. The tested technique we outline on the following pages has helped many of our clients turn their businesses around. We think it can help you, too! We have provided both an Acting and a Business perspective.

KNOW YOUR AUDIENCE

Acting Gig: Some auditions are run more effectively than others. When communication is better, the expectations are clearer. When they're not clear, you especially need to know your audience. Who you're auditioning for greatly affects both your preparation and execution, from finding material and choosing what to wear, to the energy and attitude you bring to the room.

Business Pitch: Learn as much as you can about what your "audience" expects in terms of information from you about your business. Research your audience. Get curious about the types of questions they'll want answered and the information they'll expect.

BE READY AND OPEN
TO OFFERING MORE

Acting Gig: Be ready to share another monologue, to do some improvisation, or to read a scene with someone.

Business Pitch: Be ready to answer all kinds of detailed questions about your financing and your own investment in the business. What skin do you have in the game? You need to know your business inside and out.

PLANT SEEDS—MAKE CONTACTS

Acting Gig: Know that you may not be cast right now for this role, but if you still impress the casting directors, they'll hold on to your resume and call you for another project and/or pass on your information to a colleague who has a project for which you're the perfect fit.

Business Pitch: Even if the potential client, customer, or investor doesn't sign on right away, that doesn't mean they won't ever do business with you. They may need to learn more or they may have a colleague they want to check with first. Or they may get back in touch with you in the future.

SOMETIMES THE PROBLEM ISN'T YOU!

Let's assume you have prepared by doing extensive research, memorization, and even choosing your outfit. You researched your audience—the companies or funders that'll be at your pitch presentation. You've figured out what they do and don't want. You networked with other people who have auditioned or pitched to the same group of people. You prepared by practicing and getting feedback and have adjusted accordingly. If you've done all that and still don't win the role or the new business proposal, don't beat yourself up. It may not be because of anything you can control.

The mix of people in the room can change the whole outcome, for better or worse. Sometimes the people running the auditions are more generous and giving than others. The ability to audition others well is a special skill: Can you see the potential, the fit, the skills that are there? When you're on the receiving end of a pitch, can you create an environment that brings out the best? And remember that if you don't land the audition or this pitch doesn't pay off, there's always the next one. With each audition or pitch, we're preparing, practicing, and moving closer to landing the business loan, support, and partners we need to grow to the next level.

AUDITION ABSOLUTES

The audition or pitch bears little resemblance to the job that'll follow if you get it.

- Auditions are their own art form and take dedicated practice to master—and ironically, some folks are better at auditioning than doing the gig itself.

- The person running the auditions needs to be skilled at knowing what they're looking for.

- In any audition or pitch, personality is as important as skill. Do you have the chops and are you right for the role? And do they think they can work with you?

- Do your prep and make it your own—the audition or pitch begins before you even get to the audition room or open your mouth.

- Show your passion, expertise, and commitment, all while listening to what they want in the moment.

You win some and you don't really lose any, because each audition or pitch increases your experience and visibility and often leads to something else.

SITTING IN THE "HOT SEAT": THE INTERVIEW

"We know this must feel like the hot seat." How many times have you heard that phrase when you're going into an interview?

"Hot seat" is an interesting turn of phrase when you think about interviewing. It means that the person sitting in the hot seat is being asked to answer difficult questions.

When interviewing, we encourage people to think about "being the answer" for the job. That means the interviewing team wants you to be the right fit; they want you to be the answer to their need. It's a long and arduous process to narrow potential candidates for a position. The team usually settles on the few they think will be the best fit for their company culture.

We must remember the interview goes both ways. The hot seat can be experienced on both sides of the interviewing table. Life is too short and work hours are too long for a candidate to end up in a position that doesn't fit or that doesn't bring them fulfillment. You need to assess the situation while the interview is happening. Ultimately, it'd be wonderful if it's a good fit for both parties.

It used to seem so simple. How many of us can remember back to our very first interview? Possibly it was for a newspaper route or working at a restaurant. If you were like us, you were excited to go inside the restaurant, sit down with the manager, answer a few questions, and presto ... you had the job. Not much to it, right? That was back in the day when we didn't have much awareness of what was really happening during the interview. Knowing more now allows us to help others when they're preparing for this important interaction.

We can read numerous articles that instruct us on how best to prepare for an important interview. You may look up various interviewing techniques so that you're prepared for the latest and greatest Human Resources interviewing trends. For instance, behavioral questioning allows a company to create a picture of how you've responded to certain situations in the past. You may go online and learn everything you can about the company for which you're interviewing. Also, you could call or email someone who currently works there and ask her/him a few questions.

While interviewing, realize that in addition to qualifying for the job, the team'll be looking for and assessing your executive/leadership presence. A few tips to keep in mind:

- People will be looking at your clothing. You need to wear what makes you feel best for the position for which you're interviewing.. If you have difficulty finding the right clothing, take a trusted friend to help find clothing that best expresses you.

- Footwear matters. Performers receive their shoes first, before the rest of the costume, so they can practice. This is true for us as well. We need footwear that fits the part and we need to wear them prior to the interview so they feel natural.

- We often use our hands for talking and to help us process our thoughts. If you normally use your hands to think and speak, please use them in your interview. The more natural and connected you are to the topic and to the people, the more you're going to present your best self.

- Silence is golden! Think about your answer before you begin to speak. This time helps you think of multiple work experiences to share rather than going back to the same experiences. Personally, we appreciate a candidate who gives some silence prior to the answer.

- Because this is a two-way interview, have questions for the interviewer(s) that really matter to you. Think about what you'd like to see from this relationship and be able to articulate these questions. It's easy to tell if someone has taken the time to think about this part of the interview.

Trust the universe. At times, we thought we wanted certain jobs or positions to later discover that we were saved a huge headache and a lot of stress. If you're the right candidate for the company, the seat won't feel so hot, and you'll be happy to help move the company forward with your innovation and support.

SCENE 3

CASTING

DIFFERENT PEOPLE, DIFFERENT ROLES

DID YOU GET THE ROLE? Did they cast you?

In the theatre world, performers are reminded that getting the job isn't only about who is the most qualified. In business, it helps to recognize that we are casting or being cast onto teams or projects all the time. The ability to collaborate is an element often forgotten in the casting discussion. The best fit and casting benefits everyone. It's about what skills we bring and about fitting into the group.

Do you play well with others while bringing the necessary skills? Performers make up a small part of an entire production team. Simply watch the credits of your favorite film to find that the cast is often quite small compared to the entire team that makes the film happen. Your ability to collaborate is part of the decision to cast you for a certain role, or not. Determining if you want to be part of the cast is key as well.

Get beyond hard skills, whether you're being cast or doing the casting—look at the whole person (or the whole team). Look at your teams and ask, "Who is the most appropriate fit for this project? Have I cast them well? Are they using their talents to their fullest capacity?" When's the last time you asked yourself, "How might I be better cast myself to raise the bar?"

CHEMISTRY IN CASTING: CHOOSE TEAMMATES WELL

Casting's not just for movies. In business, project managers need to cast a team that'll add value to their projects and assure the best outcome.

That's why casting directors of stage and screen are paid so well. Their job sets the foundation for a win or a loss at the box office.

Is casting any different for a company project than it is for the performing arts? No, it's crucial in both settings to find the right people for the right roles. Casting directors and project managers both know what skills and experience are required. Presence and chemistry are necessary, so both must assemble a cast that "clicks."

It's the same in the workplace when assigning specific team members to specific roles. Teams and casts are both made up of individuals but must function as a unit. Some people won't make the grade, but casting directors (and project managers) must be resolute in casting only the people who can best lead the team to success.

CREATE YOUR BLOCKBUSTER IN THE WORKPLACE

Identify the specific needs you must meet to reach the goal. For example, if the client is difficult to work with, consider assigning a team member who's good at working with challenging personalities to work with that client. If the team's goal is to close a deal, determine which team member is best at closing.

Make sure the entire cast is able to bring their "A" game: It matters who is available to be a part of the team. If a certain team member isn't available, that could shift the casting decisions for the rest of the team members.

Are the players flexible? If someone is accustomed to playing one particular role in the office, be sure they can give up that role and shift to another role if necessary. Players should also be able to identify and respond quickly when a shift is needed—it could be necessary immediately prior to going into the event, or even as the event is unfolding.

Collaboration is essential. While some colleagues like each other and get along well in general, they don't always work well together on a team. Be on the lookout for those who have good chemistry and can be productive together.

Stack the deck. Be sure to cast those who complement each other's skills. Build a team you can trust to play well together. When the team is "performing," if one team member drops something, every other member should be ready to pick it up. There's no room for "but." We can't have excuses. "Yes, and ..." is a key phrase for teams that work excellently with each other. This means we "yes" what happened and "and" it forward.

Write it down. In theatre, a casting call asks everyone who thinks they're right for the role to show up. There's a written breakdown that folks read to see if they fit or think they can fit. To create a breakdown for your business needs, write out what's necessary. This makes it much less personal and more about the job and which mix of folks is best.

Ask questions. What factors do you consider when you're putting together a team? Do your needs differ depending on whether you're pulling together a two- or ten-member team? Do members of the team discuss why they're together? They should be asking themselves "What skills do we have?" "Who should do what?" and "What 'role' am I playing?"

Consider your audience in your casting decisions. We all have a variety of skills that we bring to the workplace and to each situation. Many of us can play a variety of roles. Casting choices change depending on the needs of the specific job and the mix of people already cast. Even within a team of three people who often work together, the individual roles may shift depending on the scenario and the intended audience. Perhaps in one scenario, person A takes the lead because they've the most experience, or they have the most skill. Or perhaps they're female, and in this scenario, the audience would be most receptive to a female lead.

Define the roles. Many roles exist for each project, and sometimes cast members play more than one part. If you cast the most appropriate three folks for a particular project, figure out their specific roles. Who is the most appropriate for leading? Who is best for being ready with facts? Who should keep the meeting on track? Who'll be the active listener?

Communicate with each other, not just the audience. A team huddle ensures that the casting sticks. Take time to communicate with the rest of the cast before your event, presentation, or project. Well before the curtain rises, of course, you'll decide your team tactics and what role each of you'll play.

Equally important is determining how you'll communicate once you're in the room or on the project. Great teams, like great casts, constantly communicate and adapt to new information. If roles are clear, it's hard to be thrown—and easy for excellence to show up.

Remember: Great casting directors are highly sought after. They understand the magic of a great team. Good casting pays off at the box office, so it's a good bet that it'll pay off for your business, too. Pause. Take the moment to cast well. Then, don't be surprised by rave reviews.

KNOWING OUR ROLES

In the world of operatic or musical theatre, character roles are based on our voice type and voice quality. Musical casting directors seek a certain something in their assessment and choice of a character. Hopefully, when all is said and done, the cast of the opera or musical is the best of the best. After the cast is selected, it's time to experience the team chemistry.

As the mezzo-soprano, I'll sing duets with specific characters. My role in the opera or musical will serve a specific purpose in the cast. You can see an example of this in The Sound of Music where the mezzo-soprano is the Mother Abbess, and the soprano is the young lead.

The Mother Abbess doesn't appear in many scenes. Her status and power are felt in her inspirational aria "Climb Every Mountain." She fills a specific and important moment in Maria's life by helping her move through this life-changing transition.

Our casting, like in Opera, determines our role in a team meeting or pitch. Are you the Mother Abbess, who only needs to chime in briefly, but with great authority? Perhaps you're the lead whose voice is needed to carry the message.

Our team communication is like casting in an opera or musical. We can predetermine how and what role we play when communicating with clients. Business teams can be more flexible than casting for a specific voice type, so we don't always need to play the same role. One team member may have a more compatible communication style for a specific client and it's our task to figure out what people are more dynamic and in which roles.

- Ask the question before each client interaction: Who is best cast in each role for this client?

- Is a more assertive approach or a gentler approach needed in this communication and what team member is needed for each of these?

- Do we have an understudy ready if a team member has an unexpected emergency?

- Is there a member of the team that fits the musical theatre swing role, meaning they're versatile and highly skilled and can step into any role at any given time?

- Do you know why you are in the role you're in? What skill or skills make that role the best fit? How does that change how you interact with the others?

By thinking about our team casting and the roles that each member plays or can play, we create a more innovative approach to our client interactions and open the possibility for landing more business.

COLLABORATION IS CRITICAL

You first experience collaboration when that tiny spoon, filled with creamed peas and mashed turkey, comes toward your face. The spoon moves here and the mouth moves there. Sometimes like a game and other times a miscalculation of time and space.

Collaboration remains as vital now as it was back then. Think about it. How many hours of our professional lives do we spend working with others in a meeting, on a project, or in a presentation? At times, collaboration comes easily, and at other times ... we find peas all over our face.

As much as we'd like to be born with it, skilled collaboration takes practice. Jazz musicians know this better than anyone. They know that the talent of the individual doesn't matter unless they practice how to play together. To deliver a musical experience that sells tickets and puts an audience in the seats, musicians must learn to be aware of one another ... give cues, pick up on cues, play riffs that fill in all the right gaps, improvise with flair, and step in confidently when their solo comes. They do all this because they know their collaboration is vital to the musical experience and overall performance.

The musician's style of collaborating can work for all of us, no matter what field we're in.

We can create our own presentation orchestra during our team meetings or our client presentations, regardless of how large or small. As co-presenters, we have the ability to take our audience to new heights. By deciding which portions truly demonstrate our strengths, passing off the baton to each other, and always having our co-presenter's back, we can move the tempo, increase the volume, come into the conversation when it's appropriate, and cut off at the right times for our team members to run with the presentation and shine.

Musical practices can provide examples for us to follow:

- Talk through the score (presentation) prior to playing the notes. It's important to have a keen sense of where the music is going.

- Know which part you're being asked to play. Are you the first clarinet or the second? It makes a difference in the delivery.

- Know the cues. Will you use the subtle head-turn of the jazz pianist to the bass player, or will it be placing a pen at the top of your paper to show you'd like to enter the conversation?

- Listen to those around you. Jazz musicians know how to listen for the important line. Not every line is as important as the melody. The same is true for us—sometimes we get to take the lead and other times we're there for support.

- Begin and end strong. The beginning and ending to a musical piece are important moments in a score. The audience will remember how a piece begins and how it ends. It'll truly leave a lasting impression if you focus on the beginning and the ending of your presentation.

Collaboration will provide exhilarating moments for your audience, just like a well-orchestrated and delivered piece of music. Gather your musicians, study the score, listen to the music, and intentionally create a memorable presentation.

SCENE 4

YOU THE PERFORMER

COMFORTABLE IN YOUR OWN SKIN

PERFORMERS SPEND YEARS training in various styles, using physical and mental tasks to develop skill and craftsmanship of body, voice, and use of language. This focuses them on how to manage being real and present in the moment and helps them stretch their range and ability for a successful and repeatable performance.

We all have energy that is connected with our personalities and our physical movement. When people think about us or describe us, they often will say things like:

"She's a down-to-earth person."

"He's a thinker."

"There's no tying them down. They have a lot of energy."

When we speak or present, our energy informs our delivery. As speakers, we usually want to be "real." For us, a person is real when they're comfortable in their own skin. When they're comfortable with their topic and are comfortable with themselves, their message and presentation style become more dynamic because they're real.

Real = Comfortable being Uncomortable, and when these equate, our audience can relax to listen more closely, more deeply, and hopefully, with more openness.

INTUITION = ALIGNMENT FOR BOLD COMMUNICATING

How does trusting your inner guidance system affect how you show up personally and professionally? A lot! For thirty-five years, I've trusted my intuitive voice with clients and students, and it has helped guide my teaching, coaching, and how I facilitate the workshops I host. My goal is to use it to help move my clients forward in their communication in the boardroom and the office.

It hasn't always been easy, and my guess is that the same holds true for a lot of people. So here are two essential questions to ask:

Are you aligned with your intuition?

Are you listening equally to personal and professional insight?

If you're like me, you've found it easy to believe the outside voices of friends and family, even when their voices countered what your gut was telling you. For years, I allowed myself to be told that my intuitive feeling was an oversensitive reaction to things that weren't exactly as I perceived them to be.

These comments made me feel my perception was slightly off. Sometimes, other people's comments and perceptions made me question if my intuition was off a full 180 degrees. The fact that I denied my own observations and awareness eroded my sense of self.

Not only was I not listening to my gut, I was fully agreeing that my gut instincts were completely wrong.

Danger! Danger!

If you've had a similar experience, you know that trusting the opinions of others and letting them override your own instincts isn't a good idea. In fact, when it happens to me now, a thumping feeling starts in my gut and triggers a big siren in my head.

If others have questioned your inner compass, and you feel that you're disappearing—or worse, disintegrating—cultivate that siren in yourself. Does it sound easier said than done? Thankfully, three things that shifted simultaneously enabled me to restore my guidance system.

I moved away from relationships that were causing

me to question my own knowing.

I moved out of a bad personal relationship.

I moved out of a poor-fitting job and work environment, and some family matters shifted.

This trifecta enabled me to regain contact with my gut. Once I did, I realized it had been talking to me all along; I just needed to listen.

ARE YOU COACHABLE?

It's not a new question. People ask it about athletes. They ask it about actors. Without being able to respond, "yes," you'll only get so far with natural, born-with-it talent. Coachability is an essential success mindset for performers and athletes. Without it, performers get fired and athletes can't keep up.

Coachable people are of great value. The talent element is assumed, and the label "coachable" presumes the possibility of even greater performance. Coachable talent listens to and applies feedback, is easy to work with, and is open to the risk of trying new things. They seem tuned into the distinct difference between trying and immediately or definitively adopting the new ideas. They're willing to try a new move or a new direction and then decide if it's effective. If it is, they may keep it or still try other options. If not, they toss it. And none of this comes close to having them question their talent. Instead, this is part of the process of having talent and keeping the development going.

Excellence is tied to exploring and learning new techniques or variations on a technique. Each of us can always get better.

As a communication coaching company, we've seen the answer to this question greatly impact progress, success, promotions, and the ability to thrive.

COACHABILITY IN COMMUNICATION AND PRESENTATION

Is there a negative connotation to coaching in business—the idea that something is wrong and needs to be fixed versus the philosophy of continual improvement and a need for new skills at new levels? Why would skill development in communication and presentation be any different from another skill set? Why would some seek out a golf coach, no problem, but for their job, or communication or presentation skills, they feel wary and maybe even threatened?

Even if things are going well for you in the workplace, you may realize you need to up your skills to get to the next level in this swiftly changing business arena. Coaching support seems a good choice. And then, you may hesitate—questioning, rescheduling, feeling nerves, offering excuses.

We often think we're coachable—open to improvement and learning—but are we really? Receiving coaching often means being willing to slough off a well-worn and comfortable approach and step into trying something new. Being willing to consider a new frame of mind and develop new patterns/habits can feel extremely awkward and challenging.

Are you willing to be available?

Are you willing to acknowledge that some approaches/habits are no longer effective, based on your current goals?

Are you willing to own and develop your unique strengths to become more effective and, yes, powerful?

Are you willing to risk something new, despite the discomfort of change?

Many people speak of wanting to get better and yet block coachable information. They say yes with their heads, but their hearts stay behind: blocked, stuck, safe.

We've been there. We've found ourselves feeling that we needed to adjust our management skills and get important input on how we're coming across. And we've had clients and students who have been there. We've all signed up for a class or coaching. We show up. And then we erupt with all the defenses and excuses and reasons why it is the way it is and why it works that way. Or even if it doesn't work that way, why the fact that it doesn't work is worth defending. And then there's the complete switch of topic, and before we know it, we've moved all discussion away from self, back onto the coach or onto any other external factor. We can be quite skilled at dodging good ideas that move us out of our comfort zone!

Our own learning and growth can have more to do with our attitude than the specific coach—this coming from two people who run a company of coaches, by the way.

As teachers and coaches, we have become acutely aware of our own coachable mindset and that of the clients with whom we work. We notice a direct correlation between those who seek coaching, dive in, and willingly open up to the experience and their success. They feel no threat to their skill and awesomeness by getting coached.

We need to be both humble and confident. Humble enough to know there might be a better, easier, more effective way to do something—even if you've been successful. Confident enough to risk trying new things and know yourself enough to determine whether they fit.

And finally, you have to be willing to make a commitment to changing habits and doing things a new way. The starting point is awareness.

Signs you are coachable:

- You think, "Oh, that was good but could be better"

- You observe others with, "Oh, how can I incorporate some of that in my style?"

- You seek out mentors

- You're excited by opportunities to learn

- You constantly see teachable moments

- You feel you can learn from everyone

- You realize there's much you don't know

Signs you aren't coachable:

- You've a reason why every suggestion does not pertain to what you're doing

- You find you get angry when getting coached—okay, you may call it something else: irritated, impatient, defensive

- You sign up for coaching and then never show up—literally or figuratively

- You feel like everyone's wrong

- You can easily tell what others need to work on, but not yourself

There's always something you can tweak to become more effective—in your golf swing, your singing technique, and your communication and leadership skills.

Coachable is the difference between success ... and not so much. Coachable allows you to have a sustained career or run, and not burn out on the flames of first ignition. Coaching is the difference between "that was okay" and "that was amazing." Don't settle for status quo; soar to excellence.

SCENE 5

VOICE MATTERS

YOUR PRIMARY TOOL

THE VOICE IS THE PRIMARY TOOL of the performer. It can be an asset or a liability. Performers are vocal athletes who are challenged to have control of the voice, even when the situation in the scene is meant to seem "out of control." Spending years of ongoing voice work is part of the performer's training and livelihood. Gaining more control and understanding of the voice and how it works helps improve the performer's use of this primary tool of communication in a reliable and repeatable manner. The demands are no different in the business world. With virtual communication expanding by leaps and bounds, the demands for everyone in the workplace to use their voice in some way, such us making phone or video presentations, are multiplying exponentially. Your voice matters.

THE BUSINESS OF BREATHING

Whether you're speaking to a group or just trying to be heard by your employer, employees, or colleagues, being clear and believable are key to your success.

What sets successful leaders apart from the pack? Simple as it sounds, the answer is: breathing deeply.

We know you've heard that many times before— but do you know what it really means and why it matters so much?

Poor breath use can contribute to your sound not connecting as effectively.

More importantly, but more subtly, poor breath use can cause you to present as closed off, inauthentic, and untrustworthy. We're pretty sure that's not your intention.

At ARTiculate: Real&Clear, we're committed to helping our clients breathe deeply, speak clearly, and share their authentic message—simply. After all, crafting your message effectively is complicated enough, so let's make the voice part easy.

Most of the time, our public speaking voices are just fine. But then, oddly, only when it really seems to matter in a business transaction or presentation, our voices betray us. Voice is directly connected to breath and tension. For many reasons, we switch into a different voice and communication style when stressed or the situation seems more professional. Proper breath use is the key to maintaining our real and authentic voice. That should be easy, right?

After all, we were able to wail loud and clear when we were born. We ran around the playground screaming and shouting when we were kids. And when we're with our most trusted friends and family, we most certainly laugh out loud. But somewhere along the way, we've lost touch with the ease of speaking in public.

The goal of our public speaking training for the corporate world is to help business leaders reconnect with their authentic and powerful presentation skills in order to share their messages with greater impact and success.

Let's get down to business. Sit up straight (or stand, if you prefer) and release any tension in your shoulders and neck. Tension in your neck area makes your voice sound tight and can make you seem uptight. Exhale. Our breathing is based on a vacuum. Exhale, relax the muscles around the rib cage and feel the expansion sideways as the next breath rushes in. Yes, we're made that way—exhale and let the breath come into the lungs expanding the ribs sideways. Brilliantly simple.

Warning: Many misleading descriptions and directions have been suggested for years. Like these: Breathe in your belly. Breathe in your stomach. Breathe with your diaphragm.

Note: You're always breathing in your lungs and your diaphragm is always being used. You can't actually breathe in your belly, and most business people I know won't puff out their bellies in public anyway. Use your lungs—breathing is what they're for! Breathe sideways.

All singing and speaking voice teachers and clinical voice therapists are essentially going after the same result: get tension out of the system so the breath can flow and voice can be released fully and powerfully.

In the past, as performers, teachers, and voice specialists, we've laid on many a floor and felt our hands rise and fall on our bellies. We found it helpful to explore our instrument and get a sense of release and ease.

As we work with business professionals on their voices, two things are important to note: time is short and expansion of the belly in public isn't usually going to happen. You can work with someone all you want to help them achieve a relaxed belly breath, but when they step up to speak in public, there's a good chance that their belly will be sucked in and they'll revert to a high clavicular breath. It works to keep you alive, but isn't efficient for long-term nor loud speaking because it causes tension in the upper chest and larynx, which can be potentially harmful.

Being shallow is a choice. Sometimes when people breathe, we see shoulders rise and chests puff out. This is shallow breathing, which only gets air into the top of their lungs. The bad news is that this type of breathing increases tension, rather than releases it. Again, exhale first, and let the air flow back low and sideways—allowing the ribs to expand to the side and back with the filling of the lungs with breath.

Watch your breath as you go through the day today. Notice if you're breathing shallowly. This is sometimes called "sipping" or "clavicular" breathing. There's nothing wrong with this breath as it also allows the blood to drop off CO_2 and pick up O_2 to deliver through the body. If not speaking or exerting, this shallower breath works just fine going about our day. We have a wide spectrum of use for this breathing process, from "I need air now any way I can get it," often called the freeze/fight/flight breath—which involves a quick intake that lets air into the top part of the lungs and then we're ready to freeze/fight/ flight—to the release and relaxation that allows for optimal flow and voice control.

Stop, exhale, and let the air return deeply into your lungs. See if you feel better.

Now start talking. Your voice is powered by your exhale. Your words surf on the outflow of air. Deeper breath increases the odds that your voice will be more powerful, too.

Connecting with your deeper breath, known as the athletic breath, allows you to have a tension-free voice that enables clearer more authentic communication.

BAD BREATH—BAD FOR BUSINESS

Okay, perhaps that should be "poor breathing is bad for business." Breath powers our voices, which we use for our business communication. We offer our respect and acknowledgment of the amazing voice teachers with whom we've had the privilege of working: Chuck Jones, Rocco Dal Vera, Gary Logan, Patsy Rodenburg, Catherine Fitzmaurice, and Kristen Linklater—to name a few.

Note that some of the guidance out there on blogs and websites is well-meaning, yet suggests misleading information and ideas on ways to work on public speaking.

I care about the ease of using the voice and the authentic sharing of message and voice without making it complicated. The emotional element of voice is complicated enough. Communicating is complicated enough. I like to remember that breath and voice are simple—it's really only us who get in our own way.

It's a simple process in a complex system: a signal is sent to the diaphragm to engage to expand the lungs, creating a vacuum that allows air to rush into the lungs. We let the air out, and it passes between the vocal folds, which vibrate with the airflow and make sound. We shape the sound as it travels up and out. Voice.

So what's got me all bothered? After years of teaching voice, I believe that the use of images has taken us further from the ease of breathing, far from the ease of a loud and powerful voice. We've made it complicated.

When teaching breathing, there's a historic reliance on imaging—breathe into your stomach or your belly, as we mentioned before which invokes images of expansion far below where we physiologically breathe. The release of tension in our belly that allows movement of the spine and abdominal muscles is helpful for increased space and movement for breath—and yet we're still breathing in our lungs.

And then there's the common suggestion to breathe with your diaphragm—as if breathing with your diaphragm is an option. The diaphragm is engaged in all breathing, whether shallow or deep (unless there is paralysis, and then secondary muscles must be engaged to compensate). We have no conscious control over engaging our diaphragm. The diaphragm is a flat, dome-shaped muscle that we can't touch or see from the outside of the body. What we can do is suggest a release of the abdominal muscles so the diaphragm can drop lower, freeing up more space to allow more air to enter.

Efficient breathing for speaking involves the breath dropping into the lower part of our lungs for a fuller breath. There are intercostal muscles, between and over our ribs that expand and allow our lungs to expand outward in all directions. Many of us connect with this breathing technique when we get in the stance of a sport or physical activity: skiing, biking, softball, baseball, golf, picking up a child. This is different from the high chest breathing that often involves less movement of intercostal muscles for shallow breathing. Some of us haven't felt our intercostals move in quite some time. Others of us have, but not in connection to breath.

How about: "Remember to release your abdominal muscles, so the diaphragm can drop while releasing your intercostal muscles, to allow the maximum space for the air to fill your lungs"?

Overemphasis on belly breathing, although helpful to get the breath low in the lungs, can lead to a locked or stationary rib cage. In an attempt to move away from the clavicular or high shoulder breathing, we've moved so low to the belly area that we've missed the primary location for expansion, and thus, power for our voices.

Most efficient power source: air from the lungs.

Most common sound source: air passing through the vocal folds.

Most effective voice: what's shared outside of the mouth.

Many people compensate for the lack of air for the voice by pushing from the neck. When the power source and the sound source are both in the neck, we end up with tension that can cause strain on the voice, often leading to a tight sound.

Since our voice is an important component of who we are and what we share with others, the tension and tightness can come across as closed off and/or nervous and lacking confidence.

Throughout our day, we may come in contact with a number of people. Often the shallow breath is sufficient and, in some ways, keeps us from getting too connected to everyone we meet. That can be exhausting: deeper breath, deeper connecting; shallow breath, more superficial connecting. Both are important options in our day-to-day life. Our breath is who we are. We share our breath; we share ourselves.

When speaking involves being nervous or protective, we tend to breathe higher in the chest—the clavicular breath. We are in freeze/flight/fight mode versus the relaxed breath that is more efficient and effective for speaking and often happens when we're feeling comfortable. Our job as speakers and trainers of speakers is to be able to access the relaxed and powerful breath on demand in order to share our message with authority and authenticity.

EXERCISES TO HELP FEEL AND FOCUS ON LUNG AND SIDE BREATHING

Sit down and lean over with your belly pushed against your lap. Feel your breath expand into your sides and back.

Wrap your arms across your lower chest with your hands on your side ribs. Exhale, and feel the air come back in as the ribs expand.

Run in place until you're slightly out of breath. Feel the air in your lungs move the ribs.

Simply think of an athletic endeavor—skiing, biking, softball, fishing, golfing, or picking up a child. Most of us will connect with this lower athletic breath if we simply think about engaging in the activity.

Stand against a wall and imagine breathing into it. Make a connection between your back and the wall.

Keep a journal of your breath. See if you feel better when you breathe deeply into your lungs. And see if you get a different response when you speak to a few colleagues or friends.

But if the image of breathing into your stomach or belly works for you, go for it. Once in a while, remember that you're really breathing into your lungs.

LET THE VOICE FLOW

Speaking should be easy. At least physically.

Your voice is designed to flow without undo strain or stress. If it feels as if it's hard to make your voice carry or it gets tight or caught in your throat, you may have unnecessary tension interfering.

Here's one image that can remind you to release it: your voice rides on the exhale like a surfer. It needs a flow of air like a surfer needs the wave. Too little air and the words can't surf—the words get caught in the throat and have trouble flowing out.

Let your breath flow; release the vibrations of your words and share your voice out with the world.

NOTICE THE SIGNS OF STRESS

Some habits can point to possible vocal stress. For example, the "chin lift" and the "elbow-arm pump" can indicate lack of supportive breath for effective and healthy voice flow. If you find you push forward or lift with your chin, or your arm becomes involved in sort of pumping out the ends of your phrases, you might be pushing or straining, and it can make your voice sound tight or shrill.

Be sure you're getting enough breath. Remember to exhale and let the breath drop back in—low in your lungs—to allow for a full breath, and then let the words ride on your next exhale. At the end of your phrase or text chunk, relax and let the next breath rush in, ready for the following thought to be shared.

YES TO THE YAWN

The yawn is excellent for speakers. Yawn happily and fully. We'll suggest perhaps not in front of your intended audience—but most definitely before.

A good yawn stretches the tongue, cheeks, and lips, creates space in the mouth, connects your breath, and feels good. And new studies suggest it doesn't show boredom, but instead is about cooling the brain. We just took a wonderful voice workshop led by our colleague Robin Carr, based on Lessac's work. She reminded us that using the voice should feel good—and it can start with a good yawn. Yawn, stretch, get the cobwebs out, and awaken to spring— let your voice be heard!

Yaaaaawwwnnn...

DON'T YO-YO

Let your words land. Connect with the other person. Picture your words arching away from you and landing on the other.

Careful of yo-yoing where you send the message out but pull it back right at the end. It makes it difficult for your listener to hear the whole message. Follow through all the way to the end. Be brave. Be bold. Believe in your message and connect to your listener!

DON'T LET THEM CHANGE
THE CHANNEL

As a speaker and/or leader, your speaking voice is essential. But is your audience listening one moment, and then, click, they aren't? Are they changing the channel on you?

Think about the variety of listening options we have in our homes and cars. We can choose from traditional radio, commercial-free radio, and several HD stations, on top of our own picks that we download and stream. The selections seem endless. If a song or a voice comes on that we don't like, we can just change the station and channel surf until we land on something that meets our needs.

With a book or podcast, if we find the voice

annoying, or if we can't understand the speaker, we probably just turn it off—the content doesn't matter if we can't hang with the delivery.

Business presentations are the same. Even though we aren't in a car or at home with the ability to change the station or turn off the sound altogether, we may still find our minds wandering away from the message. If the presenter's voice is harsh, high-pitched, or rough and rumbling, we might be annoyed enough to leave the room. It can be frustrating if we can't understand what a speaker is saying, or if we get lost in a boring monotone. We may still sit there, and yet, have switched to a totally different channel in our minds.

Either our voices can be used effectively so that our words are easy to listen to and understand, or ineffectively, with poor tone of voice, poor placement of voice, lack of variety, and other bad habits. Vocal production is as important for your presentation as your visual deck or message. And the sound of our voices and use of our voices are under our control, far more than we sometimes assume. If you spend all that time on your visuals and your words, at least seek out feedback and tips on the vocal presentation.

Don't give them an excuse to change the channel on your meeting, message, or presentation!

SCENE 6

BODY MATTERS

VOICE IS PART OF A
COMPLETE SYSTEM

THE PERFORMER'S WHOLE BODY is trained as a part of communication. It's commonplace to learn about posture and how to align the body quickly for efficient use. Having an optimal physical alignment has a ripple effect on other areas, such as voice and, more subliminally, tone and attitude. Performers also learn about body movement, the most primitive and instinctive form of communication. Culturally, society tends to overlook the unstoppable reading of the posture and body movement once speech is added. The way you stand or sit in any moment gives your audience, client, or boss a very particular impression. The performer is trained to have a heightened awareness of the impact of their physical instrument. Don't undersell yourself from only the neck up. The whole body impacts communication, even when you're communicating virtually.

COMMUNICATING IS A WHOLE-BODY AFFAIR

Have you ever had a chance to see voice-over actors or singers in a recording booth? Arms, legs, heads, hips—everything is moving in connection to the message. Their bodies are fully involved even though only their voice will be heard in the end.

In years of teaching voice-over, one of the first things Hilary does is to give permission to the performers to move, groove, and get their bodies into voicing the text. Once the body is connected, the authenticity, sincerity, and real feel of the message or musicality is more clearly expressed, with breath and prosody.

It's tough to communicate with only our heads. Calling people "talking heads" points to the lack of human connection. Studies have shown that the use of hands facilitates getting our thoughts organized and ready to share. They help us think! Elvis's hips helped him connect to his message and voice.

The most effective leaders connect with their teams because they're aligned and engaged both physically and emotionally. They get it: communication involves their whole being showing up and being present.

That kind of commitment to full-body involvement in our communication has huge benefits for our clarity of message, from running a meeting to sharing a keynote, whether we're one-on-one or with an audience of hundreds.

Yes, some of this is about nonverbal communication and is also an element of a bigger, more engaging picture.

When we speak, our voice, breath, thoughts, message, heart, spirit, and body are all interconnected and interdependent. When we edit or segment ourselves, we interrupt the energy flow and lessen our effectiveness.

Studies on the connection between voice and movement have shown that each and every time, the two elements are significantly interdependent. The greater the freedom in movement with the body, the easier it is for the full use of the voice with projection and resonance.

Performers study movement as part of the whole-body training they go through. It's far beyond being able to dance. It's an understanding of where we are in space. Being able to embody our whole physical being. Connecting fully to our breath and then to the release of our voices. Showing up and being fully in our bodies and present in order to connect with our audience.

Public speaking and presentation are whole-body experiences. Even if sitting. Even if virtual. Even if only the voice is involved. Because a full, healthy, engaging voice is a full-body experience as well—aligning and engaging your whole physical and emotional self to show up fully for the most impact.

Accept the invitation to move, and get your groove on!

DANCE—JIGGLE →DO A LITTLE MOVE

Do a few dance moves on your way down the hall. Bring your whole body along to meetings and presentations. Have a little extra hip sway as you wash your hands. Find a private spot, put on your headphones, and move as only you can.

Or forget the headphones, play your music out loud, and move, wiggle, sway, groove—fifteen seconds of glorious all-out legs, hips, arms, and head movement; your voice will be free and you'll rock it!

Or, if nothing else, you'll have a great deal more fun.

BODY BEFRIENDED AND ENGAGED PREPARATION TIPS

- Roll shoulders back and exhale, allowing the air to flow back in with ease.

- Feel your legs under you, fully supporting you.

- Wiggle, sway, swing, jump, and let the breath flow and be easy, and smile.

- Do a little dance while speaking, sharing your message, in the privacy of your own space. Feel the freedom and release.

- Acknowledge the ease of voice and breath with full-body engagement.

- Be brave and step out fully present—with all of your fabulous humanness connecting and expressing!

Now, hold your space, knowing you're aligned and fully engaged, and share your message.

BEWARE THE HEAD THRUST

At times, it's completely appropriate to share only part of what we're experiencing—just our thoughts, just our intellect, and not our full emotions. For example, we do it when we say to someone, "Oh, excuse me, repeat that one more time." Sometimes we do this at home when we say, emphatically, "I really need the trash to go out." Sometimes when we argue, we jut our head forward and off of our shoulders as well. It's as if there's no room for emotion in the argument.

I was an actor in New York, and I was having vocal trouble. I went to this great voice teacher. One of the first things he said was, "You know, you should really get your head back on your shoulders." Later that week, I was at one of my five jobs, late at night. I was doing data entry seated at a desk and working on a computer. I was thrusting my head forward. I heard my vocal teacher telling me to put my head back on my shoulders, so I aligned my head ... and tears started to flow. Then I shot my chin forward again, and the flow of tears shut off. As I moved my head and neck backward and forward, tears flowed— on, off ... on, off. I realized that alignment allowed my breath to connect me to my emotional core. The breath that connects when we're in alignment is the essence of who we are. The breath and alignment promote an authenticity that we share with our voice. This authenticity is essential to connected and clear communication. With the alignment of breath, voice, head, and body, a person and her/his message are believable and trustworthy.

The first dimension—aligning our voice, nonverbal behavior, and our actual message—increases the success of our communication being clearly understood.

The second dimension—aligning our head with our heart and spirit—allows us to show up as a whole person and feel more confident, impassioned, and energized.

The third dimension—aligning our self and our teams with a clear purpose and vision that is also aligned with our values—creates a powerful force to inspire others, move quickly, and exceed goals.

SCENE 7

THE SCRIPT: YOUR MESSAGE

WHAT TO SAY

IN THEATRE, the message is set, as in a script, or it's impromptu, as in improvisation. The performer learns how to choose the tools in their toolbox to communicate in a realistic and believable fashion using solely the words that are chosen for them by the writer, or as needed in an improv scenario. Speaking doesn't always take out the ambiguity that may be evident in the written form alone. Performers try different approaches to speaking the same message to test various outcomes. They rehearse or practice each scene or chunk of text on their feet, out loud, to hear how their approach, either vocal and/or physical, is working. Maybe it's better to be sitting at a table to give this intense message rather than standing at the front of the room. Or maybe I need to use a conversational and gentle tone rather than announcing something impersonally on a microphone. The only way to find out what works is to try it on. What you say and how you say it are both essential to the landing of the message.

THE "SHAKESPEARE PROBLEM"

Let's take a look at some of our hypercorrection choices that muddy our attempt to communicate. When we hit or emphasize every word equally in a phrase or sentence, it's more difficult for our listeners to follow us.

One of the best ways to guide our listeners to understand the meaning is to increase the prosodic (or musical and rhythmic) vocal choices we make while speaking. We want to differentiate our words from one another so that they have varying qualities in rhythm, pitch, tone, and stress. We use prosody to elevate or highlight the most important word, the operative, in a phrase. MANY GRAPHIC DESIGNERS UNDERSTAND THAT WRITING IN ALL CAPS REMOVES THE VISUAL CUES THAT HELP US READ AND MAKES IT SEEM AS IF WE ARE SHOUTING

OR AT LEAST THAT EVERYTHING IS IMPORTANT. The same thing can happen with speech when we stress all syllables and words equally. Sometimes we at ARTiculate: Real&Clear dub it "the Shakespeare problem."

When theatre students are learning a Shakespeare line or monologue for the first time, they tend to equally emphasize all words—it is Shakespeare, after all, so everything must be important! Yet, even with Shakespeare, perhaps more so with Shakespeare, the operatives are key to help the meaning pop for the listener.

Take a look at this example from Romeo and Juliet:

> "But, soft! what light through
> yonder window breaks?
> It is the east, and Juliet is the sun!"

Shakespeare's verse, most often iambic pentameter, helps a performer hear where to place the vocal emphasis.

Theatre students learn to scan the text for these clues. Shakespeare actually makes our jobs pretty easy; the meaning of the speech is clear from the meter, whether regular or irregular in pattern. Both hold clues. Books and whole courses of study about this exist—we are only looking at one simple idea. In Romeo's line, the important words, or operatives, are given lift by the rhythm of the iambs, or beats.

We naturally can feel that we emphasize: soft, light, yon, window, breaks, is, east, Juliet, and sun. Next we figure which of those helps with our meaning—usually trying to only have one or two operatives per line. We need all the words, but a few guide the meaning more strongly. Try reading the line by emphasizing the italicized words.

> "But, *soft*! what *light* through
> yonder window *breaks*?
> It is the *east*, and Juliet is the *sun*!"

The meaning is fairly clear, right? "Hey, shhhh! Wow, that's a gorgeous girl looking out that window. Juliet is so beautiful she looks like the sun, rising from the east!"

Now try emphasizing the words that are italicized. It's harder to understand the meaning.

> "But, soft! *What* light through
> yonder window *breaks*?
> *It* is the east, and *Juliet* is the sun!"

The same is true of contemporary public speaking. And yet, we've found that in public speaking, people often hit the non-operatives in a stiff manner.

We often don't have meter in contemporary speech to tell us which words to emphasize, but we do know what message we are trying to communicate.

"The prices for our products have risen over
the past year."

What we often hear that makes it hard to follow someone's message is an equal emphasis on all words while in a monotone voice. With that in mind, we need to highlight the few words in each sentence that are most important for getting our message across and hit them with different prosodic values to make them stand out and sing.

And a final thought: Most of us do this naturally when we're chatting with friends. The shift to the "Shakespeare Problem" seems to happen when we switch into what we assume is our "professional voice."

SCENE 8

REHEARSAL

MAKE TIME TO PRACTICE

REHEARSAL IS PRACTICE. Performers, like athletes, recognize that rehearsal is essential to achieve a repeatable and skilled performance. Just like any athlete goes through intense training before the season starts, getting the body in optimal shape and learning the ins and outs of the game, a musician, dancer, or actor goes through the same process for each project. Rehearsal takes time and allows for an ample discovery process for the performers so the product can be of high caliber and high impact. If the rehearsal process is too short, the quality of the product can be compromised.

The safety of the rehearsal environment is key. Ideally, a rehearsal "space" is a place where performers can float and "test" various ideas, both literal and physical, with commitment and not worry that they'll make a wrong choice. In this trusting environment, an actor will often find that the most interesting choice is rarely the "safe" emotional choice for their character, but often the riskier, more courageous choice. Interesting choices lead to high impact and engaging performances. In an effort to discover the most dynamic choices and make them seem natural and real, the performer rehearses. During the rehearsal process, the actor also learns to deal with small deviations from the expected, causing them to be more at ease and robust in their performance.

EFFECTIVE MOVEMENT

Remember, when you speak, your body is there to help connect you and your message to your audience.

You have essential, change-making ideas and information to share. Perhaps you're in a meeting or giving a presentation. No matter the setting, you need to bring along your whole body to the task. Any good idea needs and deserves your full involvement, as does your audience in order for the message to be more swiftly and easily understood.

As usual, the tricky part is the how. How do we move effectively? What if you feel odd moving? What's right?

What is effective movement?

Effective movement is movement that's directly connected to our message and doesn't contradict it. When we're aligned with voice, nonverbals, and message, we send one coherent communication. Then our verbal message is enhanced, clarified, and reinforced by our physical movement.

This is different from choreography.

Choreography is specifically connected with dance, and literally means "dance writing." We don't need to be scripted. Simple movement in response to our thoughts is perfect. We may have to reconnect with our natural gestures and movement, or learn to trust that they're appropriate.

In theatre, such movement is called "blocking." This term comes from the days when directors used small blocks to represent performers as they planned stage movement.

A director's goal in blocking a play is to make the relationships and the story clear to the audience—for it to make sense. As speakers, we want to use the same process and think about how our physical movement will clarify our message for our audience. How we move in space, interact with it and impact it, all send strong nonverbal messages, and we want those aligned with our verbal message.

If a director's blocking is good, it seems natural and spontaneous. It appears to spring from the needs and desires of the character in that moment. All the movement seems honest and supports the story at hand. Speakers who bring that same organic, natural feeling to their movement on stage connect more strongly with their audience and are more easily understood.

Often, if a speaker's movements become too practiced and tied to each nuanced phrase, it becomes too much, too cumbersome, too mannered, too fake.

BE WARY OF DISCONNECTED MOVEMENTS

Sometimes blocking can seem off-rhythm. The words and movements are almost syncopated. And the movements are often quite literal in reference to the words being spoken. We often identify this as old fashioned cheerleading movement.

READY (clap!) OK! (fist in the air!)

Our blocking as speakers is best if it's in response to our audience.

Performers on stage are in dialogue with the audience. A character in a play is in dialogue with the other characters on stage—and the choice of movements is directly related to getting what they need from the other performers. The same must be true of the speaker.

If a speaker is focused on herself/himself, they'll appear to be nervous and simply pacing, or on the other end of the spectrum, they can appear to be parading themselves. To speak effectively, we want to move in response to the audience and how they're reacting to what we're saying. We move toward or away, provide gesture or stillness, depending upon the audience's needs.

TO MOVE OR NOT TO MOVE, THAT IS THE QUESTION

Should I plant my feet?

Well, yes, if that's the best connection to your audience. Don't plant your feet if it makes you feel cut off from the audience. Also, yes, because grounding oneself at the outset provides a beginning point for the audience. They know the presentation is beginning.

Should I move?

Yes, if it connects you to your audience. No, if it's about you and your needs. Physical movement needs to have engaged, purposeful meaning and should flow like it does when in conversation with a friend.

Should I go out into the audience? Is that better?

It's better if the audience needs that, but if they

need more to see you, then stay where you can see them. Walking in the audience does not mean better connection with the audience.

In a meeting versus a large speaking venue, is standing better than sitting?

If it's about the audience, yes. If it's about you, no—and oddly enough, standing isn't in and of itself about the person standing. In actuality, standing is deferential. Do you respect your audience enough to stand? Or is it about you and your embarrassment about taking the focus that keeps you seated? The latter isn't as helpful to your audience.

MOVEMENT MASTERY TIPS

Be a border collie: move on stage in direct response to the audience to keep them engaged and connected to you. Avoid wandering or pacing. That's about you and your nervous energy and not the audience.

Let your hand and arm gestures flow. Let them move to help you form your thoughts and share them with your audience. If they're enhancing your message, they'll not be too much.

Warnings: the "Flight Attendant"—parallel movement of your hands and/or arms up and down—isn't effective for your audience. Hands shouldn't be more enthusiastic than your voice because they can become distracting. Unilateral hand and arm movement is generally more organic than hands in unison, unless you're showing how big the fish that you caught was.

Know and own the space. Fill the space with you, your energy, and your ideas!

IMPROVISATION

Improv for business is like ballet for football—the high achievers realize they need cross training for outstanding performance.

For speakers, managers, team leads, and all who have to communicate with others, improv skills are essential. And we want to make a clear distinction that improv isn't simply "winging it" or "talking off the cuff."

Improv is being present and flexible in the moment: listening and responding to the needs of the situation. Being excellent at improv takes practice.

Why improvisation? Why are business schools incorporating improv into the curriculum?

In business, it pays to be nimble with our thoughts, decisions, and responses. Improvisation is about learning to be in the moment, quick on the uptake, and flexible.

Business training realizes it has a great deal to learn from the arts. Improv troupes and jazz musicians understand that improvisation is about knowing your subject so well that you can move without a script, handle variations, and play with embellishment while still having the tune recognizable.

In business, listening is absolutely essential. Improv seems like it can be all about the quick comeback or retort. Yet, phenomenal listening skills are the foundation to that response. What do master improv actors and highly successful business people have in common? They excel at listening and observing.

ISN'T IT ALL ABOUT TRYING TO BE FUNNY?

Seeing improv shows seems like it's all about games, about being clever and funny. Sometimes improv is funny. Not always. And in most good improv, being funny isn't the focus—it's simply a result. Some of performance improv can have that comedy element to it. Most often, that's because the performers are magnifying life moments, and life is funny.

One of the first rules you learn in improv is that you don't try to be funny. If we try to be funny, we often fall short. Funny gags kill the energy, and the laugh that it causes often sacrifices the work of the other team members. Gags are short moments designed to draw attention to one moment or to the character. In a classic scenario, if two actors are playing mother and daughter, and the mother character offers, "Oh, honey, I'm so proud of you finishing your first day of school!" and the daughter retorts, "You're not my mother," there's almost certainly a laugh ... and then the scene dies. It goes nowhere. Forward movement of story was sacrificed for the moment of glory, for the laugh. If, instead, we let real-life moments unfold, then that interaction tends to be much funnier. Business is the same. Business owners are using improv to learn to feel the importance of working as a team with focus on the whole. That "group mind" leads to success. Learning to be flexible and responsive to the moment is key to achievement in our fast-moving society.

Humor is its own specialty and there're many experts who speak, write, and train on humor.

When would you use improv in business and speaking? In any transaction when you need to listen during communication, to be flexible with decisions, or to go off script—improv helps us improve. Think about it. We all speak extemporaneously most of the day; no one gets up in the morning and scripts everything they'll say that day.

This demonstrates how truly gifted we're at improvising, speaking extemporaneously, and responding in the moment.

THREE ESSENTIAL BUSINESS TIPS FROM IMPROV

The basic tenets of improvisation are called rules or aphorisms: "pithy observations that contain a general truth." A few of our favorites include "yes, and," and "there are no mistakes, only gifts," as well as "how to make your partner look good."

"Yes/and" has become a universal phrase to move us beyond the re-directive, "no, but" or "yes, but." In improv scene work, we agree with our scene partners to accept a suggestion and build on it. In doing that, we move a scene forward. Constant "buts" can be funny, as in a gag, yet the scene hits the wall.

"Yes/and" invites creativity and collaboration. Take note of how often you and those around you use "but" when "and" will work as well, or in many cases, be the more correct choice.

We tend to use "but" because it makes us feel safer and more in control. It stops motion. "But" makes it clear that we have a different idea. When we use "and," it can seem like we're agreeing with what was just said, when in fact, all we want to do is disagree. By substituting the word "but" with the word "and," you'll avoid a lot of unnecessary, and perhaps unintentional, conflicts and move the conversation forward.

When we as listeners hear "but," it often makes us feel a little defensive, even if the information affirms what we had said. That little word has a great deal of sway. Use it wisely.

Believe us, it'll take practice!

Improv can help us give up the need to be perfect. Everything that comes to us is a gift. We can't make a mistake. This allows new ideas to flow and frees our mental resources. We can hear our partners more easily. We can be in the moment.

In a meeting, in a presentation, in a pitch, trust what comes, even if it's unexpected or unplanned. Embrace it as a gift versus panicking in the moment, as if it were a "mistake." When we do this, amazing things transpire.

All for one and one for all. It truly makes a difference. From years of auditioning and running auditions, it continually amazes us how apparent it is when someone is truly committed to their acting partner and making them look good. It's equally amazing to see when they are not committed—when they are all about themselves—and how quickly their performance looks poor, unskilled, or unprofessional.

In business, it's the same. When we make our colleagues or clients look good, we all win. In speaking, your audience is your improv scene partner. It's about them and making them look good.

Now, take the next steps! Go watch some improv in your town or city. Notice the yes/and. Watch the team accept the gifts and move the energy forward. Watch them make each member look good!

Then, think about taking a class yourself. Each troupe or school can have its own personality and style. Find the one that works for you.

Improvisation classes and workshops hone the skills of listening, being in the moment, and knowing when to respond. These are skills essential to good business practice. Your business presentations will benefit, your teams will benefit, and your interactions with others will be forever improved.

PRACTICE MAKES PERFECT

Most of us understand that practice matters in sports, arts, and business. What prevents us from doing the practice we know will up the level of our performance?

"Winging it" is not an option.

Actors, musicians, dancers, singers—even improv actors—rehearse. The USA Women's Soccer team certainly practiced before winning the World Cup. Successful business professionals hold preparation as a top priority. They understand that if we want to kick a fifty-four-yard goal, we have to be prepped and ready. We don't know what's going to happen in the moment of the actual show or meeting, yet practice has us prepared, honed, and tuned in to the situation and our fellow players.

If we know this, then why do we avoid it? Time constraints? Increase in performance expectations? Do we make it too intense or the expectations too high?

Promise #1: You'll end up saving time.

Promise #2: You'll have an increase in output and get more done.

Even a few moments of prep will pay off. Here's how:

MIND

Get your mind in the success mode—negativity or "realistic" mindsets eat away at our success. Know your success, see it, and live into it. Weed your mind garden of little phrases of defeat and doubt, perhaps disguised as humility.

Walk through your scenario and information in your head.

TIME

Do not give away that rehearsal time—don't let it get eaten up by other priorities.

Build rehearsal time into your overall planning. Snag little bits of time during your commute, while walking the dog, while showering. Bits and pieces are useful.

ACCOUNTABILITY PARTNER

Ask a trusted friend to let you practice and give you feedback.

BODY

Have a pre-presentation and/or pre-meeting ritual. Michael Phelps ran through the same routine before every race. Getting in a routine can help signal your mind and body that "yes, now we go."

Physically repeat, repeat, repeat. Then mentally and physically connect the dots between sections. For example, when I enter the room, I do this. When I start the meeting, I do this. When I approach the stage or lectern, I do this.

Rehearse in the shoes and/or clothes that you will wear during your performance. Your shoes inform your balance and grounding, and your clothes represent who you are.

THE CONTENT

Beginnings and endings are very important. Know how you're starting and finishing—know the in and out.

Record your content. Play and listen to it, then play and repeat it out loud. It doesn't have to be repeated back word for word (unless you are an actor with a formal script). Focus on thought-to-thought, idea-to-idea.

Learn your content in segments. Connect the segments. Work the sections—not just the whole piece over and over. Cover the segment with a piece of paper, and then scoot the paper down when you get it right. Repeat.

If you've a lot of content to deliver, write each segment by hand on index cards. The physical process of writing the words helps the memorization sink in. If you're a visual person, color-coding helps; e.g., each section or segment of content is a different color. You can use highlighters or colored index cards or paper. If you're musical or auditory, think of each section as a different instrument or song theme.

Work the hardest sections until they flow with your authentic voice and breath.

Work through it using only vowels and then add the consonants. This exercise helps you keep the breath connected and recognize the emotional content versus the intellectual content.

Run through your content out loud with anyone

who is willing to listen. Run it again. And again. Speaking out loud is key. Practice it out loud even if you are alone. Things are different in your head than out loud.

Run through your content while taking a walk, folding laundry, or doing something physical. The physical activity helps the content get into your body. The more it's in your body, the more it becomes second nature.

THE REHEARSAL OF CHAMPIONS

Audio record yourself—sound only. This can be quite different from video recording. Listen back for the clarity of message and the musicality of your voice. Do you have vocal variety that's connected to the message? Does it enhance the meaning for the listener? Vocal variety for vocal variety's sake is more hypnotic than helpful.

Video record yourself and ...

Watch with the audio off (and your harsh self-judgment off as well!). Notice your body, feet, arms, hands, head, and facial movements. Are they varied or are they repetitive? Is your pacing or other movement more about your own comfort than the audience's understanding?

Watch the video with audio on and see how you

connected your message to your verbal and nonverbal communication.

It's said that the game is won before the players hit the field. Presentations are the same way. As with performing, your preparation determines your outcome. Make the time.

Your success is in your hands.

SCENE 9

OBJECTIVES

WHAT YOU WANT THE AUDIENCE TO TAKE AWAY

ONE OF THE WORDS you hear most often in the craft of acting is the word objective. The objective is what we want to accomplish. It's where we want to go in a conversation, scene, or full play or movie. Losing sight of the objective can make a tangential idea eclipse the main idea. When a performer lets an objective guide communication, they provide a strong, clear, focused message and journey for the audience.

PREPARE TO NAIL YOUR OBJECTIVE

I often look at a note I carefully inscribed in a notebook more than thirty years ago. It says:

"Nail Your Objective: By what means, for what purpose, and to what effect?"

It is circled and highlighted and attributed to my fabulous acting teacher, Carol Rosenfeld. An addendum from her simply says: "Objective needs to be strong so there is somewhere to go."

In acting, your objective needs to be taught and practiced and honed and constantly refined. You need to consider: Is the objective strong enough? Does it drive you?

The reason is obvious: You need to know what you want. To what effect are you speaking? Without an objective, there's no direction in which to go. And, without a "super objective"—the big-picture reason that answers the question "why"—there's no purpose!

Plenty of authors and even entire businesses teach us to focus on what motivates us, and how we can harness that knowledge to be more successful.

One key tenet in our acting training is to identify and commit to an objective. We repeatedly tell our students, "Don't just walk around saying your lines! Have an objective. Know what you want. Know why you want it." When you know that, the scene comes alive. Without it, the scene falls flat.

How does this same approach apply to the business

world? By what means, for what purpose, and to what effect are you communicating? That's the key.

THREE TECHNIQUES TO NAIL YOUR OBJECTIVE

- What do you want your audience to walk away with? Why are you even doing this? Nail that down first.

- Find a verb that gets you excited to start the meeting or talk.

- Believe, commit, and go for it!

Take a moment before you enter any meeting, write a presentation, or pick up the phone to call someone, and ask yourself: What's my objective? Why am I calling? Why do I need to speak to them, and why do I need their time and their input? Know specifically, not vaguely.

Once you know, make sure your objective has power and energy with a specific verb. Find verbs that matter to you. Some folks will say, "I'm leading this meeting to deliver some information"—ugh!

Or, "I'm giving this presentation to update the team"—ugh! Get specific and energized; make it sexy!

Choice A: Speak the verb. "I'm firing up my team." "We're celebrating how this policy is going to change our bottom line." Choice B: Embody the verb (fire them up or celebrate their value). "Your input is critical in order to move forward."

Be engaged, and engage others. Use the action words that resonate with you, and you'll draw in your audience.

Pause first, and then accept the thanks you'll receive from colleagues for using their time well.

By clarifying the objective, an actor is empowered on stage and brings the performance to life. In business, the same approach will empower your team to focus. Not only will you see improved results when you clarify your objective, but you'll be present, connected, and committed. And, you prevent yourself and your team from wasting time and money by prepping the following: by what means, for what purpose, and to what effect?

TACTICS MAKE STRATEGIC BUSINESS SENSE

If we know what we want, there are a variety of ways to get it. Sometimes, we get a little fixated on one way and neglect all of our other options.

In acting, we look for a variety of tactics to use

when pursuing our objective. A character seeking the love of another may overtly pursue, threaten, ask another to speak on his/her behalf, joke awkwardly, etc. This gives variety to our character and our character's journey.

If you ever watch football, you know the coaches have huge playbooks full of tactics. They cover their mouths on TV so the information is kept secret from the other team. They call them plays. We call them tactics. We also follow a playbook to plan how we're going to go to where we want to be, and what we're going to do to get there.

For instance, if you need to get downtown to a theatre performance, you consider various tactics to arrive at your objective: the theatre. Tactics available for your consideration include: drive, walk, take the bus or light rail, ask someone to drive you, and hop on your bicycle. All of these tactics come with pros and cons. Each runs up against different obstacles. Things are always in the way of getting what we want or need. Obstacles are everywhere!

Being aware of tactics allows us to be nimble. It allows us to be aware of all of our other choices when something isn't working.

In communication, recognizing the different tactics including tone, pauses, information order, word choice, and so on, can completely alter the outcome. Whether keynoting or running a meeting, talking on the phone or having an intense one-on-one conversation, agile use of subtle or overt communication tactics leads to greater success. Yes, these may seem like small choices, *and* they can move our agenda forward.

If your forehead is sore from banging it against the same wall with no response or the same ineffectual response, step back, look at other options, and try another tactic for getting what's on the other side of the wall in front of you.

Tactics are needed to keep pace with our everyday business challenges. It's plain, good business sense.

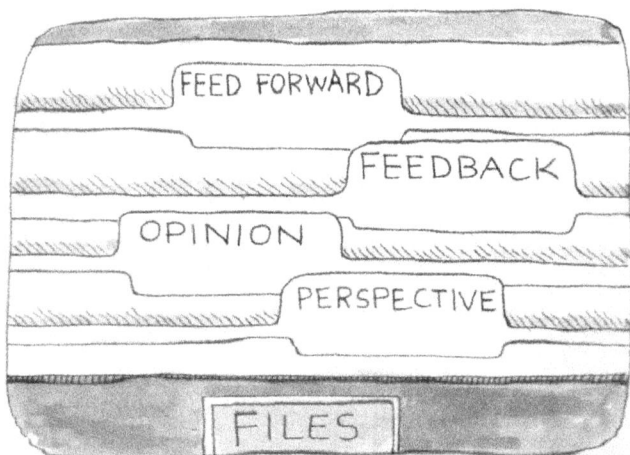

SCENE 10

NOTES AND FEEDBACK

PERFORMANCE IS A LOOP

NOTES ARE ESSENTIAL for securing an excellent final product. The performer learns through training how to receive and use feedback in the same way a director learns to monitor and give useful feedback to the performer. When both the director and performer give and receive feedback in a non-threatening manner that targets the process/actions of the character, the end results are more quickly found than with an oppositional/ argumentative manner. The performer's *choices*, and not the performer, are the topic of useful feedback.

CHOICE OF WORDS

When it comes to giving feedback, we've noticed an interesting thing ... words! We may know what we intend to say, and we may know what we intend for it to mean, but have you ever noticed when the words we chose didn't convey what we really meant? We need to think about what we're going to say and think about how the words could be heard. Think about the person who'll be hearing these words, for the first time, on the receiving end. For instance, someone said to me the other day, "Thank you for the feedback." I had to think about these words for a minute because, in my mind, I wasn't giving feedback, I was just offering an update on a specific situation. That person heard it as feedback. Let's remember that our words matter and can create a different world for the receiver.

TRUST THE COLLABORATIVE PROCESS

"That's bad. That's just bad." I can still hear the director's voice giving feedback on the scene we had just rehearsed. That's the way it is for performers. Performers receive feedback. It's all part of the process. Granted, this was not, seemingly, very useful feedback. Obviously, a little more specificity would have helped. And yet, we knew the scene needed some work, so we dug in and did it. In business, we need the same attitude.

Performance art is collaborative. There's an expectation that opinions of what does and doesn't work will be shared. And it's completely subjective. That's a given. This cycle of feedback and adjustment leads to amazing experiences for audiences if the members of the group can listen and trust that the best outcome happens when we consider how others are hearing or experiencing our presentation. Theatre relies on this collaboration and co-creative process.

Feedback is essential to any living and growing organism. Without feedback, we stagnate and die. Your brain is constantly receiving feedback from the body, and in receiving it, adjusts a whole host of physical and neurological messages in response.

Feedback is also essential in our professional careers, as well as in our personal relationships. When I mentioned giving feedback to a very accomplished colleague of mine, her response was, "Oh, you have to be tough or have thick skin." How can we change that perception for ourselves? How do we encourage feedback and keep an open mind and receptive attitude? How do we encourage it as part of a collaborative process toward a shared goal? Trusting the process, and trusting the goal is a shared one, are essential.

A few suggestions on empowering the receiver of feedback:

1. Feedback is part of the benefit and power of the collaborative process. When you create a trusting and open conversation, both the presentation and your skills will be better for it.

2. Sometimes the giver of feedback is not as skilled as we'd like. The receiver gets to choose whether to remain present to sort through what is helpful or say that they're full for the moment.

3. You need to prepare yourself to receive feedback. If you say that you'd like to get feedback, be ready for it. Listen. Simply receive it, and resist the temptation to give reasons or excuses about why you did this or that instead.

4. Accept that getting defensive doesn't help. Any comments you receive their comments as a guide to clarify your message. If they misheard you, misunderstood you, or completely missed something—that's important feedback. Instead of letting them know they made a mistake, receive their comments.

5. Remember all feedback comes through the filter of the person giving it. Even if you don't agree it can provide helpful information.

Always respond to any criticism by saying "thank you."

6. Always respond to any criticism with curiosity.

7. Remember: You set the boundaries of how much feedback you're able to receive. You can say no or enough at any time during the feedback conversation. Even in a setting where it has been established that you'll be receiving feedback, you're free to set your boundaries (i.e., in the workplace or otherwise.)

8. If you do find yourself getting defensive, simply say, "That's plenty, thank you." You can try again another time.

Don't mistake polite flattery for meaningful feedback. If you're only getting affirmative feedback, you aren't learning everything you can. If you truly want to grow, ask other folks for their input. Keep in mind it's about *collaboration*, not just about the one giving or the one receiving feedback.

I was blown away by a colleague who invited four highly-trained, highly-critical, and highly-opinionated speakers to observe her presentation and give feedback. For almost two hours, she sat and received detailed comments on what was and wasn't working. Not once did she become defensive. If she needed clarification, she asked for it. If she thought it would be helpful for us to understand what she was talking about, she gave clarification. It never came across as defensive. Needless to say, she's now my new role model. Her presentation improved, not because she was at all bad before, but because she got insightful input and perspective that made her already effective and great presentation even better. That was collaboration! She trusted the process.

Imagine: What if you could hear all the things that are working, then hear some things that aren't working, while continuing to keep in mind those that are working? Wouldn't that be wonderful and productive? If you receive feedback on five fantastic things that are working, and one suggestion for something that could be better, the one suggestion for improvement doesn't in any way negate the five. Feedback doesn't have to be difficult to hear and receive. We have the ability to invite criticism as part of our process and recognize its power to help us grow and thrive.

LISTENING

A foundational element of communication is in the listening—on both sides. There are countless articles on the importance of effective listening in business circles. Meeting a client's highest expectations can't be accomplished unless you've listened to their needs, concerns, and all the minute details of your interactions. Likewise, if you walk into a musician's or actor's class or rehearsal room, you'll hear the same directive over and over: "Listen. You're not really listening."

Acting and music require the kind of deep, relaxed listening that uses your mind in a different way than just "hearing" what was said to you. It requires that you mindfully devote your attention generously and completely to the other speaker, with no concern for what you planned to say next or what may be on your agenda. Uta Hagen, one of theatre's most famous and respected acting teachers, wrote, "We listen with our entire being when we are engaged in truthful dialogue." This kind of full-body, full-sensory listening is quite rare in real life, so that's why actors work on it as a technique ... and business benefits from listening, too.

SCENE 11

SETTING THE STAGE

BE AWARE OF YOUR ENVIRONMENT

WHERE WE ARE MATTERS. Scripts start with establishing where the action will take place. Reading a script or seeing a play with no "where" will leave the audience in a void and confused, the message lost or muddled. The environment impacts the message on stage or in a movie; and even in a radio show or podcast, the sense of environment is established by sounds or directly stated specifics to guide the audience. This is the same in business, whether running a meeting or sharing a keynote: the space matters and impacts the communication. Don't underestimate windows and lighting and how crowded you feel or how tight the room is.

THE VERISIMILITUDE OF
VISUAL PRESENTATION

Theatre has a supporting set; presentations have supporting visuals.

Have you ever asked, "What's the verisimilitude of my PowerPoint presentation?" Well, of course not! "Verisimilitude" is a huge word used most often in the theatrical and musical worlds. It's the appearance of truth—otherwise known as the ability of a play to be believable. It carries with its use an artistic call to enhance creativity and expression without losing the truth of the story.

Sure, you can put together slides to go with your presentation. Or, you can take the extra time to go beyond the simple facts and explore the verisimilitude of the message.

Librettist Lisa Kron, at the 2015 Tony Awards, shared her real live dream with the audience during her acceptance speech for *Fun Home*. The verisimilitude of her dream of a house that has rooms yet to be discovered awakened her audience to an imagined reality. Her particular vision moved us to see the world of professionally produced theatre in a new way. Calling us to finally see other rooms that have been there all along, she relayed a truth that expanded our emotional connection to the situation, without calling us out or scolding or sharing "too much" emotion. Like Lisa Kron, our visual presentation can move our audience beyond the average acceptance speech. It can truly inspire and guide our audience visually while we communicate our message verbally.

When we sit down to create our PowerPoint partner, we need to ask the questions:

- What's the purpose of the visual part of this presentation?

- How many key concepts will it have?

- What do I need to contain in each section?

- How will I build the presentation so the storyline is believable and clear?

- What images support and expand the message?

Too often, visuals are crammed full of information. One slide contains too many ideas, and the storyline becomes lost. Here are a few tips to be sure your content allows for the creativity and energy of verisimilitude.

TIP: YOUR VISUAL PRESENTATION MUST SUPPORT YOUR STORYLINE

Rather than reading your slides to your audience, imagine ways to visually express the verbal content. Lead them beyond. Think about your key idea or concept and provide visual support for this idea through pictures, words, graphs, and so on.

Some schools of thought suggest there is a correct number of slides for a certain length of presentation. And there's a correct amount of time to spend on each slide. We believe that's misleading. The slide and the time spent on each slide reflects the length of thought being shared. Some are lengthier than others naturally.

TIP: VISUALS MUST BE SIMPLE AND HAVE A CLEAR MESSAGE

Too often, presenters create a slide with more than one idea per slide. Build out your deck so you have one idea or key concept per slide. Your audience will appreciate this approach, and your visual story will be clearer.

TIP: VISUALS NEED STRUCTURE

Classical plays had five acts—so should our PowerPoint partners. Create separate heading slides for your key "acts." This will help your audience follow your story. The heading slides serve as section headers so your audience can transition to what's coming next.

TIP: VISUALS MUST HAVE PURPOSE

The storyline needs to unfold through the entire production. Spend time thinking about the flow of your presentation. Every slide and section need to unfold into the next until we are ready for the final curtain.

Theatre reminds us of the impact and importance of our visuals in storytelling. Presentations are stories. We are a visual culture, and our PowerPoint partner can add different colors to our set so the reality and creativity of our message is enhanced and supported. Don't forget to give due thought, consideration, and time to their creation.

SCENE 12

THE SHOW

GETTING ON STAGE

THIS IS OFTEN what it all builds up to: the performance, the presentation. This is when all the hard work pays off. If we care about the outcome, we still get nervous, no matter how many times we've taken the stage.

Whether you are pulling together a one-on-one talk, a virtual meeting, or a speech, and whether the prep is a few moments before or months of practice and reworking—it's still a show. It matters and we don't need to lessen its impact on us to deal with it. It's all about the audience—that's what it always comes down to: them.

EMBRACE THE NERVES

You're up there, ready to speak. You've rehearsed, you're prepared, you open your mouth, and your voice sounds nothing like you were expecting it to! It's shaky, or too breathy, or overly pinched, too high or too low. Hello, nerves!

Reframe any known nervousness as excitement. You are about to play, and your heart races, your palms sweat, and you may have to run to the restroom. In sports, this is known as excitement—anticipation to play hard and do a good job. Use this same technique in presenting, reframe the same physiological reactions as excitement and play to win. The presence of nerves indicates that you actually care. Nerves are a good sign. Make friends with them; use them. Don't fall prey to assuming you're scared to speak in public when you might just be nervous. You might actually enjoy it, and that's not an admission that you're an attention-seeker, but simply someone who enjoys sharing information or ideas with others.

NERVOUSCITEMENT: NERVES MEET EXCITEMENT POETICALLY

Stop feeding the fear creature. Resist letting others convince us that we should feel the fear. Would you really rather be in the coffin than giving the Eulogy?

Of course, many of us are scared
to speak in public,
lead a meeting,
give a speech, and
talk to two or two thousand.
If we care, we are scared.

We are nervous because it matters, because we care enough to want to do a good job. Be wary of playing into the fear of your fear. As performers, we live by the adage, "no longer nervous = retire." If we are no longer nervous, we no longer care enough about

our audience,
our voice,
our message.

Stop indulging the fear creature.

Nerves—they won't go away. Don't wish
them away. Reframe them.
Embrace them.

Pause ...

Are you truly scared? Or do you not want
people to think you're arrogant?

Our society has a tendency to confuse confidence with arrogance.

Claim your nervouscitement! Nervous/excited/
nervouscitement. It's the same physiological response
in our bodies.

Hearts beat faster.
Palms get sweaty.
We feel sweaty all over.
We may get nauseated.

In certain situations, we pay to be
nervous and scared:
rides at an amusement park,
scary movies, and
extreme sports.

Yet in public speaking, we throw money at the
prospect to be nerve-free. "It should be gone." "I must
be calm." NONSENSE! Use it. Enjoy it. Because what
price will you really pay?

You lose the nerves; you lose the care. Nerves
show you care.

Defy the fear creature. There is reason to be nervous. People are:

judging,
looking,
scrutinizing, and
assessing.

People are also:

absorbing,
enjoying,
learning, and
relishing.

Humans observe and judge other humans. Humans also crave connection. Enjoy your connection to other humans and be nervous at the same time.

Enjoy:

sharing your ideas,
facilitating a meeting,
standing in front and leading,
giving an award,
receiving an award, and
connecting.

Feeling nervouscitement doesn't mean you are not aligned. You can be fully aligned, connected to yourself *and* nervous. Don't panic when you feel a rushing heartbeat. Acknowledge it and thank it. "Thanks for caring that much." Then focus on them, your audience:

Give them what they want.
Meet their expectations.
Go beyond.
For them.

If you said you loved speaking in public, be it an audience of two or two thousand, would it be that bad? Claim it! Use your voice—we want to hear you.

PRESENTATION TIP FROM AN UNGRACEFUL EXIT

Michael Bay's ungraceful and high-profile exit from Samsung's launch at the Consumer Electronics Show in 2014, bailing in his short speaking moment, was all over the news. Bay froze as the teleprompter appeared to malfunction, he hunched his shoulders, and fled the stage. Why did it get so much coverage? This event touches on the fear that so many of us have had at some point: we will freeze, panic, and have to exit mid-speech ... we will "fail."

Some of us might get panicky even reading about it. Bay came on stage seemingly nervous already—many of us would be, especially if we tend to be behind the scenes and not in front. Being nervous isn't the problem, it's how we deal with it that's the problem.

What he did do: mentioned the problem with the prompter, so he was transparent with the audience about what was going on.

What else he could have done: focused on what the audience wanted to hear (instead of focusing on himself). He could've paused. Exhaled—and then let in a new breath so his brain could function.

He could've let his host save him, as he was trying, and be present to the helping hand.

What would you add?

In the end, as is the way with media, he did get more publicity for the product this way ... but it wasn't fun, comfortable, or a choice many of us would make.

PREPARE TO TAKE A BOW

There's the presentation itself, and there's ... the bow. Have you practiced your communication bow? When people give you praise or a compliment, are you able to gracefully receive it, or do you shrug it off?

Rehearsal is an important part of performance in the musical world. Hours are spent learning the music and then practicing with our accompanist or conductor. Knowing all the facets of our music is so important that many a nightmare is created from the subconscious mind asking if we really do, in fact, know it. When the singer takes the stage, they have practiced the music, the body movement, and the bow. Yes, the bow. It's the symbolic acceptance of praise from a grateful audience.

If you dismiss the audience's praise, you're dismissing their opinion.

Take this month to resist the impulse to say: "Oh, that was nothing." Instead, practice saying a simple, "Thank you," or "I appreciate you noticing."

Watch and you'll notice your audience being wowed with your bow.

SCENE 13

FINALE

CONNECTION OVER PERFECTION

OUR WHOLE BUSINESS, at ARTiculate: Real&Clear, is about the connection of communication between the presenter and receiver rather than the perfection.

When we connect, we feel the energy shift with our audience; they lean in, they ask more questions (not fewer), we see recognition in their eyes, they may nod or take notes, and we sense they "get" what we are communicating.

It's not the perfection that matters, it's when the *connection* creates a meaningful experience.

Sharing information with others is the goal. It can be a phone call, an email, a keynote, a meeting, a thank you card, a water cooler conversation, a quarterly update—the list goes on. No matter the situation, we're attempting to convey a message so the folks on the listening side "get" our meaning and understand our intent.

So often, that attempt at communicating goes awry—we misinform, we misunderstand, we misinterpret . . . we miss.

All the suggestions we give about how to keep the body open, the hands connected to meaning, the message clear, and the breath grounded—that's all about connection and not perfection. The perfecting details of technique are simply given to help remove the blocks that hinder clear and palpable connection.

Sometimes, the audience makes a connection *despite* the monotone voice, lack of eye contact, repetitive use of hands, distracting nonverbals, and other habits we've discussed in this book.

Many of us have been moved by speeches and TED Talks where the speaker had less-than-perfect public speaking "technique." The heart and intention of the speaker were clearly received.

And yet, sometimes the connection can't make it through the distractions and miscues. The intended messages either don't make it or are misunderstood, and things can go off track.

The goal is *connection*. All the training and tricks and coaching and suggestions for clearer communication are about connection—not perfection.

Sometimes, it's the pursuit of perfection that hinders our communication. If your attempt at perfecting the perfect stance, the perfect hand gestures, or the perfect phrasing impedes connection, then it's the wrong goal.

One of our mentors said, "If you meet someone who uses his or her voice perfectly all the time, run the other way. Don't walk, run." Perfect vocal usage all the time suggests that the person is too in control and most likely hiding the truth about themselves or the situation.

Pursuit of perfection at the expense of connection is a useless show. The "perfect" messaging goes nowhere if there's no connection. Literally, the perfectly crafted email goes nowhere without the correct address. Figuratively, the perfectly crafted speech goes nowhere without the connection to the audience.

There's no perfect presentation style.

Be committed to making your connection authentic and effective—not perfect.

Then again, if the connection is authentic, isn't it perfect?

We hope this finds you freely, bravely, and compassionately sharing your voice, message, and passion with the world!

ACKNOWLEDGMENTS

DIFFERENT PERSPECTIVES and approaches grace the pages of this book. This is what gets created when two co-owners create a work of art together. Music meets theatre and suddenly there is a spontaneous combustion of insight, innovation, and philosophy of performance. Creating this work wouldn't have been possible without the support of clients and a support team.

It's a privilege to journey with clients. Clients open doorways for us as coaches into perspectives and new ways of thinking, as their lives and experiences embrace the ARTiculateRC approach. There isn't one way of connecting, and because of this, we connect with each one of them uniquely. Thank you for your perspective and willingness to explore new ways of connecting to others around you.

A support team is more than support. They believe in the process and what's being shared. They provide the "keep going" that resonates—this is a work that speaks to everyone.

Thank you for your belief in us and in the work that we get to live every day.

ABOUT THE AUTHORS

HILARY BLAIR is a keynote speaker (CSP), champion of human connection, and the CEO of ARTiculate: Real&Clear. She is impassioned by moving beyond habits and learned behaviors to uncover what is unique and authentic in individuals and groups. A presentation and speaking voice expert, Hilary is a highly regarded coach and facilitator working extensively across the globe with a variety of businesses including Maersk, Starbucks, Slalom and AWS.

Whether working on leadership communication with members of the C-Suite, or facilitating workshops using improvisation to improve communication skills, Ms. Blair's 35 plus years of training combined with her professional stage, film, and voice over career present a unique and essential skill set. She and the ARTiculate team partner with HR departments to co-create experiential learning events that activate individual presence and team effectiveness.

Hilary is certified in Conversational Intelligence and CultureTalk, trained in ORSC and a current Vistage Speaker. She earned her CSP (Certified Speaking Professional) and is an active member of NSA

Colorado and NSA National. She is also a former board member of VASTA – the Voice and Speech Trainers Association. She has been featured in the Wall Street Journal, Buzzfeed, and numerous podcasts. Hilary holds an MFA in acting from the National Theatre Conservatory and a BA from Yale University.

ROBIN MILLER, PHD supports and coaches executives that desire more credibility in their personal connection and communication with their boards, leadership and teams, as well as more connection to self. She functions as the COO of ARTiculate: Real&Clear. Her executive coaching creates transformational shifts in communication, leadership, team dynamics and conflict management. She has successfully guided boardroom presentations, high-end interviews, and team conflict resolution.

Robin's clients are among leadership from S&P Global, Slalom Consulting, Occidental, Lippincott, Gilead Sciences to Pinnacol Assurance.

Dr. Robin Miller is a credentialed ICF coach and is a certified CTI coach (Coach Training Institute). Currently, she serves as an Executive/Leadership coach and facilitates CHIEF Core groups for executive women leaders across the United States. She is certified in Conversational Intelligence (CiQ), a trained mediator and facilitator. She earned her PhD in Musicology from the University of North Texas and her Master of Divinity from Iliff School of Theology.

ABOUT ARTICULATE: REAL&CLEAR

THRIVING IN TODAY'S business environment calls you to be engaging, effective, and most of all authentic. ARTiculate works with executives and teams both virtually and in-person to improve leadership development and communication skills that unlock potential and secure success across all aspects of business.

Learn more about ARTiculateRC team and how they can support your professional, team and personal development at **articulaterc.com**.

RESOURCES

ARTiculate: Real&Clear. "Don't Give Away Your Power" on Daybreak USA with Angie Austin. April 10, 2015. https://soundcloud.com/articulaterc/dont-give-away-your-power-hilary-blair-on-daybreak-usa-with-angie-austin/s-g2iir.

BlogTalkRadio. "How to Be a Communication Chiropractor." July 29, 2015. http:// www.blog-talkradio.com/worldpositivethinkers/2015/05/12/how-to-be-a-communication-chiropractor.

Crestcom. "Receiving Feedback to Move Forward with Hilary Blair and Dr. Robin Miller, Co-Founders of ARTiculate Real and Clear". The Leadership Habit podcast. March 2021.

The Fresh Tracks. "The ART of Voice". The Fresh Tracks Podcast with Kelly Robins. February 2017. https://www.freshtrackswithkellyrobbins.com/business-tools/the-art-of-voice/

Hengst, Corie. "Five Ways to Train Your Voice to Sound Powerful." MSNBC. March 31, 2015. http://www.msnbc.com/msnbc/five-ways-train-your-voice-sound-powerful.

LaunchStreet. "The Up and Downside of Vulnerability with Hilary Blair". Inside LaunchStreet Podcast. March 2021. https://www.gotolaunchstreet.com/podcast/the-up-and-downside-of-vulnerability-with-hilary-blair/

Let's Grow Leaders. "How do I show up with more confidence?" Asking for a Friend with Karin Hurt. March 2021. https://letsgrowleaders.com/2021/03/10/how-do-i-show-up-with-more-confidence/

Shellenbarger, Sue. "The Mistakes You Make in a Meeting's First Milliseconds." *The Washington Post*. January 30, 2018. https://www.wsj.com/articles/the-mistakes-you-make-in-a-meetings-first-milliseconds-1517322312.

Shoe Fitts Marketing. "Realigning Your Voice" with Sheri Fitts. Women Rocking Wall Street podcast. July 28, 2015. http://hwcdn.libsyn.com/p/a/3/9/a394c9fafdbe386b/WRW026.mp3? c_id=9411458&cs_id=9411458&expiration=1536262499&hwt=f8a4b-4805078d2edc09e24d7bcabec 3f.

Trevor Lee. "Business Communicating and Presenting with Hilary Blair". Better Presentations Podcast. June 2023. https://www.trevorjlee.com/business-communicating-and-presenting-with-hilary-blair/